WHEN JESUS IS THERE

Richard E. Lauersdorf

Northwestern Publishing House
Milwaukee, Wisconsin

*To all those
with whom I've shared
the Savior's strength
in life's losses*

Cover art by Gary Crabbe/Enlightened Images

Scripture is taken from the HOLY BIBLE, NEW INTERNATIONAL VERSION®. Copyright © 1973, 1978, 1984 by International Bible Society. Used by permission of Zondervan Publishing House. All rights reserved.

The "NIV" and "New International Version" trademarks are registered in the United States Patent and Trademark Office by International Bible Society. Use of either trademark requires the permission of International Bible Society.

All quoted hymns are taken from *Christian Worship: A Lutheran Hymnal.* © 1993 by Northwestern Publishing House.

All rights reserved. No part of this publication may be reproduced, stored in a retrieval system, or transmitted in any form or by any means—electronic, mechanical, photocopying, recording, or otherwise—except for brief quotations in reviews, without prior permission from the publisher.

Northwestern Publishing House
1250 N. 113th St., Milwaukee, WI 53226-3284
© 2003 by Northwestern Publishing House
www.nph.net
Published 2003
Printed in the United States of America
ISBN 0-8100-1558-7

Contents

1 Surmounting walls of trouble
2 Child's serious illness
3 Chronic pain
4 Blindness
5 Paralysis
6 Age-related losses
7 Adjusting to a nursing home
8 Confidence in changing situations
9 Failing memory—Alzheimer's
10 Divorce
11 Divorce affects children
12 Infertility
13 Empty-nest syndrome
14 Runaway child
15 Disappointed by friends
16 Death of a pet
17 Job loss
18 Destruction of home
19 Economic loss
20 Imprisonment
21 Burglary—violation of safety
22 Low self-esteem
23 Fear of losing faith
24 Rejoicing in suffering
25 Training to handle loss

1

No Wall Too High

With my God I can scale a wall.

Psalm 18:29 (NIV)

How high can you jump? If my memory is correct, the world's record is somewhere around 8 feet. Just think. That's 2 to 3 feet higher than most of us stand in our stocking feet. Such a feat must take a lot of training, conditioning, and practice.

Looking back over his life, David talked about high jumping. Many were the walls of troubles, problems, and dangers he had to leap over in the course of his days. But he always made it—with the help of a faithful God.

Losses in life are like walls to be overcome. It makes little difference what the loss is. Whether our health or home, spouse or child, job or livelihood, that loss is a wall that juts up before us. It makes no difference how the loss came about. Whether by injury or disease, divorce or relocation, retirement or dismissal, that loss looms before us. The list of life's losses is inexhaustible, and the circumstances, endless. And so often each loss, especially when it's my loss, seems more than 8 feet tall. It seems higher than I could ever think of jumping.

What should I do? Should I bury my head in the sand and ask, "Wall, what wall?" as if nothing had happened and the hurt will just go away? There's not enough sand in the world to make that work.

Should I ball my hands into defiant fists and shake them at a God who doesn't seem to care? When my misdirected anger is spent, the loss will still be there.

Should I punish myself with the guilty thought that the loss would not have happened if only I had believed more? Such self-whipping only serves to increase my pain.

Or should I get busy and try jumping over the wall?

I could never do that by myself, of course. How could I train enough, practice enough, toughen myself enough to hurdle life's troubles? That would be like a little child trying to run the rigorous obstacle course used to train Uncle Sam's elite army rangers. By myself I could only tumble backward into the mud and lie there in despair. But when God takes my hand, when his strength lifts me up, when his love in Christ empowers me, we can negotiate trouble's wall together.

When Jesus is there, no wall is too high.

Prayer

Lord Jesus, take me again to your Word. Remind me that you have promised never to leave me and that your love, which paid for my sins, will empower me to hurdle the losses of life. Amen.

2

CLOSE TO HIS HEART

He gathers the lambs in his arms and carries them close to his heart.

Isaiah 40:11 (NIV)

What are we supposed to do? My wife and I look at our hands—those same hands that held our little one as she gurgled her little sounds and grinned her little smiles. Those hands are supposed to take care of her. She clutched one of them when she took her tentative first step. She didn't want to let go of them when she walked through the schoolhouse door that first time. In our arms, at our side, she always felt safe. But now we can't help her.

How little she looks in that hospital bed! How painful the needles and how threatening the machines! We don't want to leave her room, even to get a cup of coffee in the snack bar. We can hardly pry ourselves away at night, even after the medication has put her to sleep and she doesn't know we're there. But the worst part of this is the horrible feeling of helplessness, that numbing frustration that comes from not being able to protect her.

Like a sudden blow to the solar plexus, illness can knock the breath out of us. When it strikes our child, it's even worse. What can we do? Where can we turn? How thankful we can be that the Lord answers those questions. We can turn to the Shepherd who gave us our child and to whom little ones really belong. Like a powerful shepherd, Jesus cares for his own. The loving Shepherd carefully wraps the weak lambs and those recently born in the folds of his robe and carries them close to his heart. We may be able to do little or nothing for a sick child, but Jesus can do anything.

Look at what the Lord has already done for our child. While we waited for her arrival, he guarded her in the womb and caused her to grow. At the right time, he brought her safely into the world and into our arms. Even more wonderfully, at the baptismal font he gave her the life that lasts, as he worked faith in her heart and wrote her name in his book of heaven. Covered with his robe of righteousness, she was readied for life's journey and headed for heaven's shores.

Now, Lord, help us place our child's earthly needs into your loving hands. In our helplessness point us to your power. In our hopelessness fill us with your comfort. Remind us that *when Jesus is there*, our child is safe—on earth and in heaven.

Prayer

Loving Shepherd, little ones to you belong. They are weak, but you are strong. Hold our child close to your breast. Care for her as you know best. Above all, keep her safe to all eternity. Amen.

3

MEDICINE FOR AN ACHING SOUL

Be merciful to me, LORD, for I am faint; O LORD, heal me, for my bones are in agony.

Psalm 6:2 (NIV)

Constant pain can gnaw away at us. It saps strength, strains patience, and sets daily life on edge. How can I live with constant pain in my bones and joints? The doctor calls it osteoarthritis and comments that many my age have it. But that doesn't take the pain away. Nor do the pills he prescribes for me. For a while they mask the pain, but it always comes roaring right back again. The doctor also informs me that there is no cure, and that only makes matters worse. Is he saying that I'll have to live with my ailment the rest of my days? I don't know if I can.

Look at my fingers. Once they were so straight and slender. They could bend and twist—they were active all day long. Now whenever I try to hold a pen, turn a screwdriver, or handle a paintbrush, they ache for hours. Look at my knees. Once they could move so gracefully and run so speedily. Now when I sit for more than ten minutes, I can hardly get up again. And running is out of the question. Shuffling slowly forward is more my speed these days. Some nights my pain cuts like a knife whenever I turn on the mattress. Some mornings I'd rather stay curled under the blankets than face the pain another day will surely bring.

Is there no help for me? Can't the pharmaceutical companies come up with some new drug that will finally bring relief? Perhaps someday. The Creator has filled his creation with so many wonderful things that nothing is surprising. All we have to do is unearth what God has given. But until we do, or if we don't, what am I to do?

David points me to an answer. In my agony I'm to look heavenward. If anyone knows about pain, Jesus does. Not the pain of inflamed joints and hurting bones, but flesh torn by cruel nails and cutting whips. Not only pains that radiate from the troubles on this earth, but pain that erupts from the torments of hell. Oh yes, my gracious God knows, and he will help. When I'm weak, he's my strength. When I can't, he can. When the days seems too long, he helps me through. In the morning and evening, I can cry, "Be merciful to me," and he will hear.

How can I be sure? Hasn't he prepared the medicine for my aching soul? Wave after wave of hell's punishment washed over him on Calvary, as he carried the sins of the world. Now ahead of me, instead of hell with its endless torments, stretches heaven with its pain-free peace.

And all because *Jesus my Savior is there.*

Prayer

Jesus, you know how much my bones ache. Help me find relief as well as the strength to endure. When I don't know what to do, point me again to the cure you have prepared for my sin-aching soul. Let that blessed healing keep me going even through the pains of life. Amen.

4

Blind Eyes That See

> "What do you want me to do for you?" Jesus asked him. The blind man said, "Rabbi, I want to see." "Go," said Jesus, "your faith has healed you." Immediately he received his sight and followed Jesus along the road.
>
> Mark 10:51,52 (NIV)

"If only I could see again for just one day," Henry would comment. Each time I visited him, he'd repeat his wish. If only for one day he could see the gladiolas he used to tend in his garden. If only for one day he could see the church building he once cared for as the custodian. If only for one day he could read his Bible again. "Pastor," he would say, "tell those children in confirmation class to learn those passages and memorize those hymn stanzas. You never know when you'll need them."

It's hard to imagine not being able to see the sunset as it colors the sky or my beloved at my side. Not to see the joy on my grandson's face or the player speeding toward home plate with the winning run. Instead, to be stuck in blackness—morning, noon, and night.

No wonder Bartimaeus begged Jesus that day, "Rabbi, I want to see." He wanted light instead of darkness, sight instead of blindness. And Jesus—always compassionate—granted his request.

Some days—in fact, many days—I beg Jesus for the same miracle. "I want to see," I tell him. I know he hears me. I know his answers are always right. But some days I find it difficult to accept when he says no to my request. Some days I almost feel like shaking off the hand with which he guides me in my darkness.

Then it's time to look at Bartimaeus again. He received more than physical sight that day. The Savior gave him eyes of faith. With those eyes he could see Jesus as he went to Jerusalem on his divinely appointed mission of salvation. With those eyes he could see that Jesus was going to the cross also for him. Bartimaeus would follow this loving Savior down the road of life.

God, help me see what Bartimaeus saw. Though I can't see the faces of my loved ones, by God's grace, I can see the saving love on Jesus' face. Though I cannot view the beauty of the flowers, I can preview heaven's glory. Though I still walk in darkness, my heart is bright with God's promises.

When Jesus is there, even the blind can see.

Prayer

Lord, help me live with the eyes you have given me. In the darkness let me see the light of your love that leads and guides me. Above all, help me appreciate the eyes of faith you have given me. Focus those eyes on my Savior and the heaven he has prepared for me. Amen.

5

No Hope?

Cast your cares on the LORD and he will sustain you.

Psalm 55:22 (NIV)

It had taken only a moment, but it would last a lifetime. When they pried him out of the wreckage, his lower body was paralyzed. For 20 years, he had walked on his own; for the rest of his years, a wheelchair would transport him. What a burden for that young man to carry. What a future—trapped in his body, trapped by each day, and, so he thought for a while, trapped by his God.

My body doesn't work either. Nor is there any hope that it ever again will. I'm stuck in a life that's more about existing than living. I'm a burden to those around me who have to do so much for me. I'm a burden to myself. I don't like my thoughts. I don't like my anger. I don't like my constant carping and complaining about the hand God has dealt me.

It's time to listen to David again. "Cast your cares on the LORD," he said. "Your cares." Each of us has his or her own, designed to fit our particular shoulders. Before God sends crosses into our lives, he measures our carrying capacity. After the crosses have come, he works to strengthen our muscles. When the cares become too heavy, he finally removes them.

"Your *cares*," David called them. A 10-pound bag of sugar requires little muscle to carry. A 100-pound bag of salt is far different. God never promised us all sugar and no salt. Nor did he ever promise minimum poundage. Instead, he speaks of burdens that can last a lifetime and cares that can crush those who have to carry them.

"*Cast* your cares on *the Lord*," David advised. I can't lift my burden, no matter how hard I try. The Lord tucks it under one arm and carries it. On my shoulders, that care is a crushing boulder. In his hand, it looks like a mere pebble. I can't handle my cares, but God can and does.

Hasn't he already not only relieved but also removed my heaviest burden, that crushing care called sin? My sins rob me of all hope. With hope absent, I have no peace. But, in Jesus, God has given me the greatest hope of all. Through Jesus' payment for all my sins, I have divine power for all of life's cares. And the sure promise of heaven above.

When Jesus is there, life has hope again.

Prayer

Helper of the helpless, I need your help every hour. Watch over those who care for me, and bless their efforts. Watch over my heart, and fill it with the comfort of your promises. Let your salvation give me hope for life's long day and, above all, for heaven's eternal day. Amen.

6

LIFE KEEPS GOING

Even when I am old and gray, do not forsake me, O God, till I declare your power to the next generation, your might to all who are to come.

Psalm 71:18 (NIV)

I never thought it would happen to me. When I was younger, my grandma seemed so old. She'd tell the same stories over and over. When I brought the kids to visit, she didn't always remember their names. When I'd tell her something important, she'd often forget. It was no fun watching her deteriorate little by little. Every time I looked at her flower garden, once spotless, covered with weeds; her hands, once so busy, gnarled and folded on her lap; her needle work, once her favorite pastime, abandoned beside her chair; I cried inside. Each time I visited, I wondered if it would be the last.

Now it's happening to me! I can't fool myself any longer. Life now has more losses than gains, more withdrawals than deposits. The pain in my joints won't get any better. My eyesight—macular degeneration the doctor called it—will only get worse. My memory, my strength, my ability to be active, will only fade more. And I don't like it. It's no fun growing old.

I can't help thinking about what lies ahead. How long will I be able to stay in my own home? How many times can I leave the stove burners on high? How soon before I need a wheelchair or the care of a nursing home? How much more can I expect my children to do for me? How soon will they get tired of helping me? Some days I don't even want to see another day. Dying might be easier. At least then I'd be rid of my concerns, and my family would be rid of their burden.

It's time to look up again at my changeless God. I've become old and gray, but he is the same yesterday, today, and forever. I don't always remember, but he never forgets. My hands shake with weakness, but he is my strength and stay. My sins keep coming, but he still promises that the precious blood of his Son has erased their stain. The days left for me aren't many, but he keeps me focused on his eternal day. What would I do without him? May he never forsake me. Lord, please help me never forget you.

One thing more, Lord. Remind me why you still leave me here. Remind me that now I have more time than ever before in life to tell the next generation about your love. More time than ever before to pray that they know you and not forget you when they are old like me.

When Jesus is there, life keeps going.

Prayer

Change and decay in all around I see;
O thou who changest not, abide with me! Amen.

7

MY SURE SOURCE OF STRENGTH

I have learned to be content whatever the circumstances. I can do everything through him who gives me strength.

Philippians 4:11,13 (NIV)

Gabriella had been used to watching her favorite programs but now had to share the TV with a roommate. She had been a good cook but now had to put up with bland meals. She had loved the tranquility of her own home but now had to endure noise, even at night. Gone was her freedom to do what she wanted when she wanted. When I visited her that first time in the nursing home, I wondered what I'd hear.

Did she complain? Of course! I would have too. Her life had been turned upside down. Did she cry? Yes! There were tears, and I could understand why. Life as she had known it was gone, and she could do nothing about it. Did she want to go home? You bet! Wouldn't you, if you were in her shoes? Coaxing me with a smile, she wondered if there was anything I could do, someone I could call, so she could get back to her home of so many years.

Then, when I read Paul's words to her, she listened intently and slowly nodded her head. Imprisoned in Rome, Paul was writing to Christians who had more than their share of trouble in life. Yet the apostle spoke to them of contentment. He had learned from experience what counts in life. The Savior—with his pardon for our sin, power for our troubles, and promise of heaven—is life's real treasure. To have Christ is to have it all. To have it all without Christ is to have nothing.

"I know," Gabriella said. "Jesus is with me here too. I know sometimes I have to be satisfied with second best as you've just told me, Pastor. So please, if I can't be back in my own home, ask Jesus to make me content with the one I have now."

Easy for Gabriella to talk like this? No. In the weeks ahead, would she forget at times and even complain bitterly? Yes. But life would go on for her as it had for the apostle Paul. And she could be content.

When Jesus is there, believers can do more than they ever thought possible.

Prayer

Lord, I miss my home and my independence. I know I should be happy that I have a place to stay and people to take care of me. But it's not the same. Please, Lord, don't let my homesickness turn into bitter complaining. Please lead me to be content with what I have. Please keep me looking toward my heavenly home. Amen.

8

CONFIDENCE IN THE MIDST OF LIFE'S CHANGES

Since you are my rock and my fortress, for the sake of your name lead me and guide me.

Psalm 31:3 (NIV)

How quickly life can change! Enrique's surgery did not go the way the doctor anticipated. Instead of a repaired rotator cuff, he ended up with an arm he couldn't raise above his chest. Never again would that right arm turn a socket wrench or steady a rebuilt motor as it was lowered into a car. All his life, Enrique had wanted to be a mechanic. For him nothing was better than the chance to repair cars at the shop or to tinker with them in his own garage at night. Now what was he going to do? How could he live without the satisfaction that comes from making a car purr as it should? How would he put food on the table for his family? Just like that, 15 years of his life were gone, leaving only memories like so many oil spots on the concrete floor.

Change can be so threatening. It can alter my very being and affect who I am. Dealing with the present changes may be more than I'm able to handle. Trying to peer beneath tomorrow's curtain brings little relief. Like a dense mist, today's loss can fog the glasses of faith so that I barely catch a glimpse of the Lord at my side.

But he's still there. Like a rock, steadfast and sure, he's there. And I can rest faith's trembling legs on him. Like a fortress, he's there. And I can find shelter from adversity's arrows in him. He was there to lead and guide me yesterday. He'll be there to lead and guide me tomorrow. Though he doesn't always show me where we are going or how we will get there, I can breathe easier because he is my rock and fortress.

"For the sake of your name," David said to him, "lead me and guide me." That's my cry and conviction also. I know his name. It's spelled with the capital letters of his love. He's my SAVIOR. He's already healed the sin-torn muscles of my heart so that I can reach all the way to his heaven. He's my LORD. He holds not only the whole world in his hands but especially my tiny future. He's my SHEPHERD. His goodness and mercy cover not only my yesterdays but also my changed today and my uncertain tomorrow. Though I may not be able to see where the path leads, or I may hesitate to step out onto it, he will help me.

When Jesus is there, I can face the changes in life.

Prayer

Lord, so much has happened to my life. I don't know who I am anymore or what I should do. Please turn my eyes to your unchanging love. Assure me that you work all things for my good and that your plan for my future is filled with your goodness. Amen.

9

My Father Remembers

As a father has compassion on his children, so the Lord has compassion on those who fear him; for he knows how we are formed, he remembers that we are dust.

Psalm 103:13,14 (NIV)

Sometimes he knew me and at other times not. When he was having a good day, his wife would call, and I'd hurry over with private Communion kit in hand. Yet some days, by the time I sat down across the kitchen table from him, he'd look at me as if I were a total stranger.

How much like dust we are! Minds that once were so sharp, that shaped productive careers, that shared joys and sorrows can be blown this way and that by the winds of time. How soon will the medical profession come up with answers? Will they ever totally understand the causes of debilitating problems like Alzheimer's—or offer a cure?

My heavenly Father knows my condition, both soul and body. And even better than any earthly father, he has compassion on me. He knows my limitations at any given moment, and he never demands from me what I cannot give. He knows how sin has crippled and condemned me, so he doesn't demand that I shake off my sins and their debt. Instead, he sent his beloved Son, Jesus, to chop off sin's chains and cancel sin's debt.

He also knows how quickly my body can become like dust. Again his fatherly compassion shows itself. When my mind can't recall his saving name, he still remembers me by name. When I look at the Savior with blank eyes as if he were some stranger, he promises to never forget me. When my fading memory can't come up with a single passage, he again whispers the words softly to my heart. What would I do without such a Father?

And what would my family do without him? With that helpless look in their eyes, they watch my mind slowly crumble. With their faithful efforts, they hover around me. They weary with today and worry about tomorrow. How much longer can they keep me at home? How much worse can I become? How dearly they also need the reminder of his fatherly compassion for those anxious days ahead!

I may forget, but my Father always remembers. *When Jesus is there,* I belong to him.

Prayer

Lord, remind me that faith is more a matter of the heart than the head. When my mind fails, please still remember me. When my family wearies, please strengthen them to walk with you and then with me. In the Savior's name I ask this. Amen.

10

HIS BECKONING ARMS

"Whoever comes to me I will never drive away."

John 6:37 (NIV)

"It's worse than death," she said. Her divorce was final, but her ex-spouse was still very much around. When he picked up the children for his weekend, she could hardly avoid him at the door. When she went to social gatherings, she might catch a glimpse of him in the crowd. When she went shopping, she often had to duck into a store rather than meet him face-to-face. And each time, the scab on her slowly healing heart would crack again, and grief's bleeding would begin anew.

Divorce can be worse than death. After a person's death, we can recall the good things, not the unhappy experiences of the past and the resentful feelings of the present. At least with a death we can hold a funeral and visit a grave. We know that the person is gone forever and that nothing can be done about it.

But with a divorce, there's no finality. Instead, there are recurring reminders of former happiness, forgotten vows, and failure toward God. Instead, there are his friends, my friends, and our friends. Instead, I get strange looks from some in the congregation and strained conversation with others. Like a white elephant, my divorce sits there in the middle of my life, and I can't make it go away.

Thank God, he doesn't tell me, "Go away." Instead, with arms wide open he invites me, "Come. Come with your anger toward your spouse. Come with your sins that damaged your marriage. Come with your penitent tears and let my forgiveness dry them. When I said from my cross, 'It is finished,' I meant these sins too. When I say 'Go in peace,' I'm talking also to you."

Thank God his arms also carry me into the future. He doesn't drop me to the ground like an impatient parent, saying, "Now you're on your own." Instead, he walks beside me. When I'm lonely—even in the middle of a crowd—he whispers, "I'm still here." When I don't think I can face tomorrow with all its uncertainties, he assures me, "You don't walk alone." Always his arms are open to me. "Come," they promise. "I'll never drive you away."

When Jesus is there, I can go on, even though alone.

Prayer

Lord, you know my penitent tears. How sorry I am for the damage I caused in my marriage, and how much I desire your forgiveness. You know also how difficult it is to go on alone with life. Please walk with me as my Savior, helper, and friend. Please keep your inviting arms open for me. Amen.

11

LITTLE ONES TO HIM BELONG

He took the children in his arms, put his hands on them and blessed them.

Mark 10:16 (NIV)

"The only ones who gain from a divorce are the lawyers." So the saying goes. More to the point is the statement, "The ones that divorce hurts the most are the children."

Seldom do you find children who don't want their divorced parents to get back together again. Divorce upsets the lives of children, shattering not only their present but their future. How do they handle practical questions: With whom will I live? Which address is home? Who will take care of me? Who will pay for my college education? How should I react to Dad's new wife? What do I call her? Who will walk me down the aisle someday when I get married? Should I get married or will my marriage only end in divorce too?

Some of the questions are even more personal and emotional: Whom should I love more? What if I hate Dad? Whom can I trust? Whom can I really open up to and talk with about my fears? Whom can I go to with my dreams?

Of course, children long to have their parents back together. How much more simple and steady life would be.

Seldom do you find children who don't feel some guilt about their parents' divorce. Regardless of their age or how long ago the divorce occurred, the guilt lingers: "I must have done something to make them so unhappy. If only I had loved them both more, maybe they would have stayed together. If only I had tried harder." If only this, and if only that. With a rough edge, real or imagined guilt scrapes away at their hearts, leaving raw sores that can last a lifetime.

"Jesus loves me, this I know," the Sunday school song proclaims. If only I could hang on to the comforting truth that "little ones to him belong." He gave his miracle of Holy Baptism especially for children. With water and the Word, he picked me up in his arms, put the sign of the cross on my heart, and penned my name in his family register. He made me his child and, regardless of my age, loves to hold me and lay his blessing hand upon me. My parents may part company, but he remains at my side. My life may change, but his love is still the same. My future may look ever so black, but his love shines as brightly as ever.

When Jesus is there, I know to whom I belong.

Prayer

Thank you for making me your child through faith. Let the assurance that I am part of your heavenly family comfort me as my earthly family dissolves. May the blessings you bring me outweigh the losses I experience in the upsetting events in my life. Let me feel your love, and help me trust that it will never fail. Amen.

12

STILL HIS CHILDREN

How great is the love the Father has lavished on us, that we should be called children of God!

1 John 3:1 (NIV)

"You have been married how long and still no children?" acquaintances ask. "We'd sure like some grandchildren," parents and in-laws hint. "It's all my fault," we cry alone, or in each other's arms, after the specialist's report comes back. What we wouldn't give to have a child of our own. Not just to carry on our name but to fulfill the instincts the Creator has set deep within us.

How many more silent tears do we have to shed? Is it wrong for us to keep praying for a child? Is it permissible for us to seek help from a specialist? Such are the questions we ask in our deep anguish. We need some answers.

First of all, we need the reminder that no one can play God. The divine Creator has reserved for himself the miracle of beginning a new life when the father's sperm and mother's egg come together. Why he does it for one couple and not for another—sometimes for couples who don't want a child but not for those who do—is for him to answer. But we hope he understands when we ask why he hasn't done it for us.

Should we keep praying that he give us a child? He gave Rachel her son Joseph (Genesis 30) and Hannah little Samuel (1 Samuel 1) in answer to prayer. Who's to say that the Lord, with whom nothing is impossible, won't do the same for us? When he doesn't, we need to ask for the wisdom to accept his answer and to look for alternatives. Perhaps we could adopt or become surrogate parents to nieces or nephews or work with the children in our congregation, thus giving and receiving love.

Should we go to fertility specialists? God can use them to help achieve the blessing we so much desire. But we need to beware when such specialists advocate methods that ignore the sanctity of life or bypass the husband or wife as the source. Our desire for a child dare not come at the expense of disregarding God's will.

Above all, we need to remember that his ways, though mysterious, are always right for us. His answers, though hard to accept, are flavored by his love. Though we may have no child of our own, he calls us his own. Though no one calls us father or mother, by his grace we can call him our Father. In Jesus the Savior, we can see how much he loves us.

When Jesus is there, life is full of his love.

Prayer

Lord, if it be your will, please grant us the child we so desire. If not, please help us accept your answer. Calm the longings of our hearts with the answer that you are still our loving Father and we are still your beloved children. Help us go forward in life with this love. Amen.

13

WEEP? LAUGH? OR BOTH?

> There is a time for everything, and a season for every activity under heaven . . . a time to weep and a time to laugh.
>
> Ecclesiastes 3:1,4 (NIV)

"The house seems so empty," she mused. "There used to be music playing, doors slamming, cars coming and going. Now it's so quiet. I open the fridge, and it's still full. I buy milk by the half gallon and bread one loaf at a time."

Three weeks earlier they had moved their last son off to college. With pride they had waved good-bye as they walked back to the parking lot. Their son was well on his way to becoming a man. With a sense of accomplishment, they had driven away. For 19 years they had been working toward this day. Yet tears filled the mother's eyes, and a lump rose in the father's throat. Never again would their house be the same. And as the days passed, that house seemed so empty.

"Empty-nest syndrome" is what the experts call it. Regardless of its label, it's a change and necessitates adjustments. Dad and Mom are home alone again, just as they were during the first days of marriage. Life revolves around the two of them, instead of three. Daily schedules, daily tasks, even weekends are different. Sometimes the marriage needs some overdue attention.

Marriage, as planned by the Creator, is the union of one man and one woman. Each cleaves to the other, united by the glue of love. Children are a result, not the cause, of their union. Yet, over time, the glue that holds a husband and wife together can end up being their concern for the children more than their love for each other. When the nest empties, they may have to reach for the glue gun again. Now they have time for each other, time to enjoy and enrich that which brought them together in the beginning. And the empty-nest time can become the golden years of marriage.

Empty nesters can find joy in the achievements of their grown children. The time for bending the twig is past. Now it's time to watch the tree grow—and hope it grows straight. The opportunity to impart spiritual values is over. Now parents watch as grown children assume responsibility for their own souls. The parents are filled with joy as they observe how the Lord keeps his promises and blesses the faithful teaching and modeling of his Word. They rejoice even more as they look far ahead to the day they will stand with their children in God's heavenly family.

Not all loss is bad. Not all change brings tears. When the nest empties, it's a time to weep and a time to laugh. But only *when Jesus is there*.

Prayer

Thank you for the child you gave us, Lord. Thank you for working with us as we tried to raise him for your kingdom. Now help us enjoy the days we have together as a couple. Let the years ahead be rich ones for us on earth and even richer for us in heaven. Amen.

14

Perhaps Not Lost

Train a child in the way he should go, and when he is old he will not turn from it.

Proverbs 22:6 (NIV)

"We don't even know where she is," sobbed the mother. "We have no idea why she did it," sighed the father. Their quiet 17-year-old daughter had run away. When the county fair was over, the midway people had pulled down their rides, and Connie had run off with one of the roustabouts. Clueless as to why, hurting from the loss, beating themselves up with blame, the parents sat in the pastor's study. Though months later they finally heard from Connie, she never did come home. Thank God, they had another daughter, who married happily and filled their lives with several grandchildren.

What do you tell such parents? Every Sunday the four of them had sat in the worship service. In their daily lives they had walked the talk, modeling their faith. Yet this happened to them. Underneath their anxiety were deep concerns about themselves. Had they failed as parents? Could they have done more? The pastor wisely took them to Solomon's words. "Notice," their pastor reminded them, "he said, 'Train a child in the way he should go.' He didn't say, 'Make the child go that way.' Only God can do that."

When the "yes, buts" came from the parents, the pastor continued. "Ed," he said, "you're a farmer. When you want a good crop, you prepare the field well, plant good seed, fertilize, and cultivate. But you can't make the harvest come. Do you always get a good crop, and is it your fault if you don't?" Now Ed and his wife could better understand. Even as they asked for pardon for whatever responsibilities they might have neglected, they were a step closer to peace.

Underneath their anxiety were also deep concerns about their daughter. What about her faith? Had she also run away from Jesus? Again the pastor quoted Solomon's words. "He said, 'When he is old he will not turn from it.' Solomon didn't say there'd be no exceptions," the pastor carefully pointed out. "Sadly some who run away from Jesus never find their way back. But Solomon did offer some comfort. Though today your daughter seems unfaithful, tomorrow may still see fruit, which, by God's grace, will grow from the seed once planted at home and in church. Who knows?" the pastor concluded. "When eternity dawns, you may find that the child you thought was lost, really wasn't."

When Jesus is there, the lost may be among the found.

Prayer

Lord, you gave our child to us. You know how we tried to raise her for you. You know how anxious our hearts are now with our child gone. Comfort us with the reminder that you are in charge of faith and that your Spirit works through the Word. Please use the Word we have taught to bring our child into your kingdom. Amen.

15

MY FRIEND, CLOSER THAN A BROTHER

There is a friend who sticks closer than a brother.

Proverbs 18:24 (NIV)

What's a friend? Someone who still likes you even after he knows what you're like is one answer. Someone to whom you can bare your soul is another. Someone who's always there is a third. Next to a spouse, a friend is one of God's greatest gifts.

And yet friends can bitterly disappoint us. "He was closer to me than a brother," one man commented sadly. "Yet, when there was some money to be made, he undercut me."

"I told her secrets I had never shared with anyone else," another lamented. "Then she turned around and told everybody else."

"We thought we had the same ideals. They seemed to be conservative Christians and good workers for our church," remarked a disappointed couple. "Yet when problems arose in the church, they jumped right in with the troublemakers and threw gasoline on the fire."

Earthly friends come and go. They delight, but they also disappoint. That's the way it's been ever since the fall, and that's the way it always will be till the end. When someone I trusted fails me, it's hard to swallow. I have to work at choking back my sudden anger, clubbing down my injured pride, and curbing my bitter resentment. Though I may be more cautious with a new friend, I have to learn to trust again. In the meantime, my answer to the question, What's a friend? becomes, Someone mighty hard to find.

How different with my Jesus! What a friend he is! All the definitions fit him. He still likes me even after he knows what I'm like. In fact, he does more than like me. He loves me with the most unselfish, undeserved love imaginable. Though my sinful heart made me his enemy and my sinful life so often treats him like dirt, his love remains constant. "I still love you," he says. "My blood still covers all your sins. I'm still right here at your side."

What a friend my Jesus is! Time after time as I bare my soul to him, he listens patiently and lovingly. In fact, he makes it possible for me to talk so openly to him. "See my hands, my feet, my side," he says. "See how my love allowed them to be pierced for you. See what precious pardon my love prepared. Now come," he invites. "Sit down here next to me on the dock of life and tell me all your problems. Then together we'll set sail, and the seas will be calm."

No friend can love me more or be closer to me. *When Jesus is there*, I have life's best friend.

Prayer

What a friend we have in Jesus,
All our sins and griefs to bear!
Do your friends despise, forsake you?
Take it to the Lord in prayer.
In his arms he'll take and shield you;
You will find a solace there. Amen.

16

A Gift That Lasts Forever

Christ Jesus . . . has brought life and immortality to light through the gospel.

2 Timothy 1:10 (NIV)

For his birthday little Tommy wanted a dog. "I don't know," his mother said. "They can be a lot of work." But that night Tommy's dad brought home a loveable puppy. "I'll call him Patches," Tommy said, "because of his black and white spots." From day one the boy and his dog were inseparable. Where one went, so did the other—except to school. On school days Patches had to wait at the door till his master came home.

One day as Tommy got off the bus, Patches bolted through the unlocked screen door and playfully ran past Tommy, right into the path of the bus. After a sickening thud, Patches lay in the gutter, a crumpled ball of fur. Tommy had lost his good friend and for the first time had come face-to-face with death.

His parents showed wisdom when they didn't minimize his loss. Instead, they helped Tommy bury his friend in the back flower bed. They even watched as he put a crude marker over the grave. This gave them the opportunity to discuss whether animals will be in heaven. They discovered that Scripture doesn't clearly address that question. They also used this as a chance to point out the difference between Tommy and his pet—that only one of them has an immortal soul designed to live forever in heaven. They explained to Tommy that in heaven there will be no more loss or sorrow, only total joy. In order to help him understand, they suggested that heaven will be like playing with Patches all day long. Best of all, they used Patches' death to speak again to their son about Jesus. So the loss of a pet became a learning lesson for this Christian family.

"Because of Jesus we don't ever have to die," they told Tommy. "Those who know Jesus will live forever with him in heaven. Jesus came to pay for our sins and to prepare a life that never ends. Someday, as with your puppy, something will happen to us. Our hearts will stop beating, and we'll stop breathing. But unlike Patches, each of us has a soul, the part of us that laughs and cries and that lives in our bodies as if they were houses. Our souls will go to be with Jesus. Loved ones will put our empty bodies into graves, but one day our bodies will go to heaven also. Jesus will raise our bodies from the grave, make them perfect like they never were before, and reunite them with our souls for the life that never ends in heaven."

When Jesus is there, we have a gift that lasts forever.

Prayer

Thank you, Lord, for the gift of pets. They are precious gifts. When I lose a pet, I feel sad because it is no longer there to keep me company. Use even its loss to point me to the never-ending life you have prepared for me in heaven through your death and resurrection. Amen.

17

Now What Should I Do?

Commit your way to the Lord; trust in him and he will do this.

Psalm 37:5 (NIV)

"It's just not fair," Roger complained. "All these years I've worked hard for the company, even giving them many of my weekends. Now they've terminated my position. I suppose I should have seen it coming," he went on. "Sales were down and every once in a while a coworker received a pink slip. But I never thought it would happen to me."

"Now what am I going to do?" he wondered. "Where will I find a new job? Who will hire someone my age? How am I going to provide for my family, pay the mortgage, and put our daughter through college? Besides," he continued, "do you know how it makes me feel to lose my job? Like some kind of failure."

My job is a great gift from the Creator. Through my job, he not only provides for my earthly needs, he also puts purpose in my life. When I lose my job, it's as if a vital part of my being has been cut away. The days seem so empty as I wrestle with questions, like "Who am I now?" The future seems so uncertain as I worry, "Where will I find a new job?" Only those who have lost their jobs know how traumatic it can be.

David wrote about times like this. He didn't say, "Don't be concerned. Don't send out any resumés or fill out any applications." Of course the Lord wants me to use the mind he has given me. He wants me to cope with my changed life and face the challenges of the future. But when I've done my best, David reminds me, "Commit your way to the LORD." I need to remember who's really in charge of my life, including the work that fills it. I need to take my concerns to my loving Lord, asking for his guidance and seeking his blessings.

I also need to trust the Lord. What do I accomplish when I whisper only halfheartedly into his ear as if I doubt that he is concerned about me or that he cares enough even to listen? Trust means to look confidently to him, lean totally on him, and leave my concerns fully in his loving hands. "He will do this," David promised. The type and timing of his answer, I leave to him. But I can expect his answer to come. After all, hasn't he already filled my life with the blessings of salvation? Won't he also fill my life with an earthly blessing like a job?

When Jesus is there, I don't need to worry about life's necessities.

Prayer

Lord, you gave work to people as one purpose for living and one way of providing for life's needs. Please fill my life with this blessing again, whenever and wherever you know it will be best for me. In Jesus' name I pray. Amen.

18

Rich Forever

> "Store up for yourselves treasures in heaven, where moth and rust do not destroy, and where thieves do not break in and steal."
>
> Matthew 6:20 (NIV)

"We're still rich," the young man stated, even as the smoke was still trailing skyward from the charred ruins of their house. An electrical problem had started the blaze in the middle of the night. The sleeping family had escaped with just the nightclothes on their backs. Gone were all their possessions, including the memorabilia that mean so much in life. With his arm around his wife and two young children clinging to his legs, the Christian man told his pastor, "We're still rich."

Not everyone can talk like that. When a sudden storm or raging fire levels our home, we lose so much. That home is one of our greatest investments. Whether we watched it being built or bought it later, it's precious to us. That home is where our family lives and loves. We set our Christmas trees up in one of its corners and hang, not just our stockings, but our very dreams on its walls. That home is a place of security, togetherness, and joy. And yet so quickly it's gone.

So it goes with earthly treasures. Moth and rust may not be as prevalent as in Jesus' day. But there's little protection against fire and flood. Thieves may still break in and steal, regardless of security systems and neighborhood watch programs. Earthly treasures are for us to use, not to use us. God gave them to sustain our existence, not to become the reason for it. We need earthly treasures like our house. But we are not to set our hearts on such flimsy things.

Instead, we set our hearts on the Lord. What a home he has waiting for us in heaven, a mansion compared to the mud huts of this world! What heavenly riches he has already given us for our enjoyment! The richest curtains and clothing are rags compared to his robe of righteousness. The finest pieces of furniture are only sticks when displayed next to the pardon and peace on which we recline. The dearest memorabilia are like cheap marbles alongside our baptisms and his Holy Supper. "Treasures in heaven," Jesus calls them. And that's what they are—treasures that no catastrophe on earth can destroy and that no fires of hell can snatch away for eternity. His grace gives and his love guarantees the treasures that last forever.

That young man had it right. *When Jesus is there* with his heavenly treasures, we're rich forever.

Prayer

Thank you, Lord, for the gifts from your hand that sustain our earthly lives. Thank you especially, Lord, for the treasures you have prepared for us in Christ. Keep our hearts focused on the riches of your grace so that we fuss and worry less about our earthly needs. Amen.

19

DIP AND DIVE OR ONLY HIGHS?

"Do not worry, saying, 'What shall we eat?' or 'What shall we drink?' or 'What shall we wear?' For the pagans run after all these things, and your heavenly Father knows that you need them."

Matthew 6:31,32 (NIV)

Each time I get an updated report, the bottom line is smaller. I thought I was all set. My retirement nest egg was growing nicely. The mutual funds were increasing, not spectacularly but steadily. When my financial advisor analyzed my finances, he said that, barring unforeseen problems, I could live, not like a king, but comfortably in retirement.

Unforeseen problems. He must have meant events like the slump in the economy, the dive in the stock market, and corporations resorting to Chapter 11. Now look at my finances. My nest egg keeps getting smaller and my retirement further away. Thinking about my financial losses only gives me a headache.

Perhaps I should look less often at my financial statements and more often at my heavenly Father. That is the Savior's advice. "[He] knows that you need them," Jesus says. My heavenly Father knows far better than I do what I need in order to live. Food and clothing, job security, and retirement planning are all figured into his plans for me.

When I retire, he'll still be at work caring for me. Of course, he wants me to continue my efforts too. Factored into his care for me are my efforts at saving for tomorrow and investing for the future. But when I have done what I can, he reminds me, "Move over now and let me take over."

Sometimes I hear his promise and still worry. Like an unbeliever, I just don't get it. Or if I hear his words, I don't quite believe them. The pagan has an excuse. He worries about holding on to earth's marbles because he hasn't learned about heaven's gold. He tries to peer anxiously into the future, making his little plans with his little mind, because he doesn't know about the One who directs all our plans with his loving hands. Like an orphan who doesn't have anyone to take care of him, the unbeliever fears the future.

I have a Father whose love never fails and whose power always provides. I have been made his child by his saving work in Christ Jesus and his faith-producing work through his Spirit. "Trust me," my Father says. "Trust me for today and for tomorrow."

When Jesus is there, my earthly and eternal future is secure.

Prayer

Lord, teach me to leave the future in your capable hands. Help me to do what I can and then trust you to do the rest. In my times of financial loss, help me find security in the promises you provide. In Jesus' name. Amen.

20

BEHIND BARS BUT FREE

"If the Son sets you free, you will be free indeed."

John 8:36 (NIV)

How I long to be free again! To breathe the outside air, walk familiar streets, hug my loved ones. Never again to hear cell doors clanging shut or to eat in a noisy dining room with fellow prisoners. Never again to watch the clock and wonder why the hands move so slowly. Never again to mark the calendar and wish the days would pass more quickly. "Free as a bird," they say. I don't even want to fly that high. I just want to get out of here.

Even more, I want to be free from my guilt. I belong in this cell. What I did was wrong. I hurt not only other people but my God. With my sin I told Jesus that I didn't care about what he had done for me and what he wanted me to do for him. It was as if I spit in his face. When I think of him, I wonder, Does he still love me? Are his eyes blazing with anger or still gazing at me with love? Please, someone, tell me that Jesus still loves me. That his blood covers even this crime. That his redeeming work has freed me from sin's guilt and Satan's grasp.

"You don't know how much your visits mean to me," I try to tell the pastor as I ask him to come again. He doesn't look down his nose at me as if I were some damned sinner.

He doesn't excuse my sin either. When he reminds me of God's commandments and sin's curse, I squirm inside. But then he reminds me of Jesus' forgiveness, and my soul smiles. He tells me the story of the prodigal son and the waiting father—and I know what he's talking about. How glad I am that my Father still welcomes me and still wraps his forgiving arms around me! How glad I am for my freedom in Christ!

My family comes too, in spite of their inner hesitation and the inconvenience of the trip. Just to know that they care frees my spirit. They can't take the prison bars away, but they help me live inside them. They can't take me home with them, but they can bring a taste of home to me. And I can tell them again how sorry I am for the hurt I've caused. Every time they come, I silently vow that I'm going to work to make it up to them when I'm out of here again and free.

The bars still hold me, but I'm free. *When Jesus is there with his love, I'm free indeed.*

Prayer

Lord, I have sinned and need your forgiveness. Please welcome me back with your forgiving love. Please help me pay my debt to society, even as I long to be free again. And when the gates open and the bars are gone, please keep me faithful to you. Amen.

21

MY SECURITY BLANKET

Keep me safe, O God, for in you I take refuge.

Psalm 16:1 (NIV)

Thieves had ransacked her apartment. They had torn off the lock, trashed her rooms, and taken what they considered valuable. Those things she could replace. Insurance would cover most of the cost. But what about her feeling of security? Though she could move to a new apartment in a more secure neighborhood, she would still wonder when it was going to happen again. "I feel so violated," she said. "I don't know if I'll ever feel safe again. I wish I could find a security blanket like the one I clutched as a little child."

For her it was an apartment break-in. For another it might be a rape—by someone known or unknown. It might be an act of terrorism, like the dreadful and death-filled destruction of the World Trade Center towers in New York City. Or something else. Just like that, my sense of security is gone. The confident "It can't happen to me" becomes "I wonder when it will happen again." And I start searching for some security blanket, something to hold on to through anxiety's long night.

I might need professional help to untie the tight knot inside me. I surely want my family and friends at my side to unlock the choke hold worry puts on my life. It may take more time than I expected, or that outsiders ever thought necessary, before I can pick up any semblance of my life again.

Most of all, I want to reach for God. I need him to be my security blanket. Unlike the blanket of my childhood, he's more than just a soft cloth that lulls me into a false sense of security. He's real and so is his help. With his almighty arm, he'll hold me close to him as he whispers, "There's nothing you and I can't face together. You and I are a majority of one against any odds." With his loving arm, he'll hold me even closer as he reminds me, "I gave you Jesus for the sin that violated your soul and snatched away your eternal security. Now trust me to freely give you things like security and peace." With his all-seeing eyes, he is able to see into the future. "I know already where I'm going to take you and what I'm going to do for you. Just hang on and let me carry you."

Anxieties don't disappear overnight. Beating back such giants takes a lot of hard work. But when Jesus is there, I can breathe more deeply and rest more easily.

Prayer

Lord, how am I ever going to feel safe again? How can I stop looking over my shoulder, waiting for something bad to hit me again? Raise my eyes to you. Help me trust your power, your love, and your wisdom. Help me trust you to hang on to me in the present and to hold me in the future. Amen.

22

Not Junk in His Eyes

"I [the Lord] have summoned you by name; you are mine."

Isaiah 43:1 (NIV)

"God made me and God don't make no junk," the message on the T-shirt proclaimed.

"I wish I could believe that," she sighed as she read the words. How much like junk she felt. In her family she was always the odd one. Relatives overlooked her. Parents put her down. Perhaps they didn't mean to or didn't know any better. But many a night she wet her pillow with her tears. She had hoped that marriage would change those feelings. And at first her husband did treat her like his beloved bride. But before long, he was criticizing her for what she didn't do, and carping at her for what she did. "Still junk," she thought, as she made her way through each day.

Situations may vary, but the problem of low self-esteem is serious. It sags the shoulders, saps the spirit, and takes the spring out of life. Who wants to be down all the time? Who wants to look into a mirror, expecting to see only junk?

There are no easy answers for the loss of self-esteem. Solutions come slowly, requiring hard work by the individuals and those close around them. For Christians, the road to self-esteem begins with the realization, "God made me, and he does not make junk." Better still, it begins with the realization, "God remade me in Christ Jesus and turned me into his treasure."

Isn't that what God says through Isaiah? "I have summoned you by name," he reminds me. At my baptism he came seeking me and wrote my name in his book of heaven. As I make my way through the ever-present heartaches of life, he comes repeatedly and calls me by name. Just as he spoke to Mary on Easter morning, so he asks me, "Why are you crying?" Just as with Mary, his love dries my tears, even those caused by my feeling of worthlessness.

"You are mine," he also tells me. Others throw me aside like so much junk. He handles me carefully as a cherished treasure. Not because of what I am or what I have done, but because of what he has done for me. Because of Jesus, I am his own child, dear to his heart, destined for his heavenly family. Because of Jesus, I am a precious jewel, polished by him on earth to shine in his eternal crown. Though some days I feel more like a lump of gravel than his precious stone, more like some forsaken orphan than his dear child, that doesn't change what I really am. Self-esteem begins not with what others think about me but with what my gracious God has made of me.

When Jesus is there, I am valued and loved.

Prayer

What love you have shown me, precious Savior, by making me your child and heir of heaven. When I feel worthless in life, remind me of this blessed truth. Help me face the struggles in my life, assured of your love and armed with your acceptance. Amen.

23

Don't Let Me Go

> Consequently, faith comes from hearing the message, and the message is heard through the word of Christ.
>
> Romans 10:17 (NIV)

"I think I've lost my faith," the young man sighed. He was sitting, head in his hands, in the pastor's study. Everything seemed upside down. His life was messed up. God seemed so distant. But worst of all, his faith seemed to be vanishing out the back door.

The pastor listened. He didn't cluck his tongue in disapproval or dismiss Steve's concerns as frivolous. Instead, he pulled a paperback copy of the New Testament off the shelf and handed it to Steve. "Here," he urged. "Take this home. Read through Luke's gospel and Paul's letter to the Romans and come back next week."

When Steve returned, he was ready to talk.

"Faith is God's gift." The pastor reviewed what he had once taught his former confirmand: "At birth the heart is like a fist clenched in defiance and unbelief. It cannot reach out for or grab onto the salvation that comes through Jesus Christ. All it can do is knock that good news away. Through the gospel, the Holy Spirit must unclench that fist and turn it into the opened hand of faith into which Christ's riches can be poured. This he does through the Word."

"Once opened by the Spirit," the pastor continued, "the hand of faith can clench shut again. Those who hold Christ's treasures can let them slip through careless fingers. That's why, even though God promises to keep us 'strong to the end' (1 Corinthians 1:8), he also warns us, 'Be careful that you don't fall!' (10:12). If we drift from the Word, we're like a patient who pulls the intravenous line with its life-sustaining fluid out of his arm. We've cut ourselves off from the Spirit, who works through the Word, not only to create but to sustain faith within us."

Steve smiled. "I know why you gave me this New Testament," he said. "I read it. All of it. And I felt better. It was as though Jesus were talking right to me. As though he were saying that I still belonged to him and that he wouldn't let me go. Can I keep this book?" he asked. "I need to read it more."

Now it was the pastor's turn to smile. "I was concerned about you," he said. "But I didn't think it was too late. When people worry about losing their faith, it's a sign they haven't. The ones who stop worrying about their faith are the ones I'm really concerned about."

When Jesus is there through the Word, his Spirit will be there also, sustaining faith within us.

Prayer

Lord, you know how weak my faith is, how I fear that I am forgetting you. Turn me to your Word so that your Spirit can pump new energy into my heart. Help me read and reread the good news of my salvation. As I read, may your Spirit work his miracles in my heart. Amen.

24

We Just Can't Lose

> We also rejoice in our sufferings, because we know that suffering produces perseverance; perseverance, character; and character, hope. And hope does not disappoint us, because God has poured out his love into our hearts by the Holy Spirit, whom he has given us.
>
> Romans 5:3-5 (NIV)

Does Paul really expect me to believe his words? How can I rejoice in suffering? What hope can I gain from my loss? Regardless of how I measure it, loss still feels like loss to me. Something has smashed down on me or something has been snatched away from me, and life will never be the same. I can rejoice in the good things God provides and look forward to the heavenly glory he promises. But rejoice in sufferings? I just don't know.

But let me read Paul's words again. "Suffering produces perseverance," he said. A sailor who's never gone through a storm doesn't know how to react. Sea legs come from standing on a wave-swept deck at sea, not one anchored calmly at the dock. Setbacks in life teach important survival skills. When God tests me with loss, he's trying to toughen me for the obstacle course called life.

"Perseverance [produces] character," Paul continued. When the storm finally passes, the believer is no longer a raw rookie but a seasoned veteran. Now he knows God's promises, not just as some words he once memorized in confirmation class but as a power that he witnesses in real life. When I see God in action, I learn to lean on him. That's what Paul means by character, the ability to look to and lean on the Lord in the day of loss.

"Character [produces] hope," Paul concluded. For me, hope is not some fanciful musing, not some baseless dreaming. My hope is as solid as God's love for me in Christ, the rock on which my hope rests. Such hope does not disappoint. I won't be left holding the bag after the dust settles. The one in whom I trust is a God of such love that he gave his only Son as my Savior. The one on whom I rest my hope is a Father who through that Son has prepared a room for me in his house. The one on whom I lean in my loss is the King who wields such power that he can turn loss into gain by using it to shape my life and strengthen my hope.

When Jesus is there with his love, I just can't lose.

Prayer

Jesus, Savior, pilot me
Over life's tempestuous sea;
Unknown waves before me roll,
Hiding rock and treach'rous shoal.
Chart and compass come from thee:
Jesus, Savior, pilot me. Amen.

25

Train Hard, Run Straight

Everyone who competes in the games goes into strict training. They do it to get a crown that will not last; but we do it to get a crown that will last forever.

1 Corinthians 9:25 (NIV)

"What does it take to play like you?" someone once asked a famous violinist. "Training," he replied. Though he was a renowned veteran of the concert stage, he still practiced at least ten hours a day. He was much like the Olympic athletes of yesterday and today. Behind the laurel crown of Paul's day and the Olympic gold medals of today stands lifelong preparation.

So why do I think I can handle life's losses with little or no training? How can I automatically expect faith's muscles to handle any problem, lift any weight, or jump any hurdle? Don't I know that people of faith don't just suddenly get that way? Doesn't it make sense that, like an athlete, I need to train constantly for life's contests?

When life's losses come, I'll still grieve. I'll never be a super-Christian, one who can take anything and bear everything without flinching. I train so that though life's losses may slow me down, I can still keep running the heavenly course. I train so that my faith can still keep breathing, instead of wheezing with doubt or gasping with anxiety.

When life's losses come, I'll still search for meaning. The road to heaven is steep enough and the pace hard enough without additional obstacles. Why does the Lord put potholes on my course and rocks in my way? Surely he doesn't want me to stumble and fall, does he? No, but he doesn't want me to take my eyes off the finish line either. How easily I might relax the pace or allow the world's goals to distract me if the race were too easy! How easily I might lose the crown if God didn't cramp my muscles at times so that I realize I need to train harder!

Above all, when life's losses strike, I'll reach for his strength. When I think I can't run another lap or draw another breath, I begin to realize how much I need his power. When Jesus runs with me, pacing me, even pushing me from behind, the finish line draws ever closer. But not without rigorous training.

Those who train in his Word learn to trust his promises. When life's losses come, they keep on running all the way to heaven.

When Jesus is there, I can train hard and run straight.

Prayer

Run the straight race
Through God's good grace;
Lift up your eyes and seek his face.
Life with its way before us lies;
Christ is the path and Christ the prize. Amen.